The GReen BOOK OF POeTRY

An anthology of children's poetry about the environment

**We do not inherit the earth from our ancestors
We borrow it from our children**

Native American Proverb

Published by SCEMES Ltd

Registered Offices: Meriden House, 6 Great Cornbow, Halesowen,
West Midlands, B63 3AB, UK

www.scemes.com

First Published: 2007

Printed in England by WPG Ltd, Welshpool

ISBN: 978-0-9557871-0-2

The views and facts expressed by the contributors within this publication are not necessarily those held by the publishers. The children's contributions, in every way possible, remain unchanged and have been reproduced as they were written.

Profits from the sales of this book will be donated to the charity Plan, one of the largest child-centered community development organisations in the world.

The Publisher's policy is to use paper manufactured using renewable timber produced on a fully sustainable basis.

Foreword

This selection of poems was written by school children as part of a National Poetry Competition on the theme of 'The Environment'. The competition took place in the academic year 2006 to 2007, the year marked as the Government's year of action to improve awareness on environmental issues.

From my experience, it appears that young people care deeply about the environment and want to do their bit for it. They realise that they, above everyone else, will have to live with the future consequences of the actions we take today.

This book only serves to reinforce this impression. It contains a wealth of insightful and affecting writing that shows young people really understand the complexity and urgency of environmental issues far more than we sometimes give them credit for.

The pupils have revealed a high level of understanding for this complex ecological problem and we can only hope that their engagement with it, through this competition, will encourage future sensitivity to the needs of the planet.

Everyone who participated in the poetry competition that led up to the publication of this book is to be commended for playing a part in keeping the environment at the top of the agenda.

Congratulations are due to all the pupils who contributed to this book, I hope it will act as a reminder of the sincerity they had at this young age to issues which affect us all and they will continue to engage with the world around them and understand their responsibility to protect it.

The Green Book of Poetry works to show anyone who reads it that with future generations the world will be in good hands.

Phil Woolas MP
Minister of State for the Environment

Acknowledgments

This anthology of children's poetry first occurred to me when we were considering the plans to implement our National Poetry Competition. The thought occurred to me that should the competition catch the imagination, then it would be nice to publish a selection of entries as an anthology and donate the net proceeds from sales of the book to a charitable cause.

This publication has achieved the first part of our ambition and it remains to be seen how successful we are in raising some funds for our chosen charity, Plan. Plan is one of the largest child-centred community development organisations in the world, helping children and their families in 46 of the poorest countries to realise their full potential.

Many people have made a significant contribution to the success of this project. It began with Laura Hughes' idea for poetry as the ideal Competition medium through which to develop the writer's subject theme of 'Environment'. We are grateful to both David North and Felicity Woods who successively saw through the implementation and the completion of the Competition.

Along the way, we have enjoyed the constant support of many people who assisted in spreading awareness within schools about the Competition aimed at KS2 students. In particular I would mention Cliff Jones of the National Primary Headteachers Association who is always willing to take time out of an over busy schedule to offer advice.

Thanks to our judges: Bill Laar, Phil Woolas and Johnathon Porritt, who gave freely of their time to read the many entry submissions, they remained enthusiastic from start to finish.

The final editing of this Anthology was the work of Felicity Woods who has managed to combine it with her final studies at Edinburgh University for her M.A in Literature. In this task she has been ably assisted by Kirsty Walsh who has brought her design and organisational skills to see the project to completion.

Finally and most importantly, all our thanks go to all those special people who made the whole thing possible, the children, together with their teachers, head teachers and parents. They have made this Anthology possible. They embraced this competition completely and through their poems took the opportunity to give us all a special insight into their hopes and concerns, their thoughts and ideas about what the environment means to them.

And we must listen, because the future belongs to them.

Robin Mathias
Managing Director, SCEMES Ltd

Contents

Poetry is the record of the best and happiest moments of the happiest and best minds

Percy Bysshe Shelley (1792 - 1822)

A Beautiful Scene?

Jake Regan, Aged 11

A giant redwood,
Standing tall and proud.
But soon is destroyed,
From a passing acid cloud.

The powerful roaring ocean,
A delicate grassy bank,
A worried father with a tiny son,
All ruined from an oil tank.

The blazing sun seems to get hotter,
But really it's our mess.
A tiger rug and bear fur.
Stop building more and build far less.

Animal population's smaller,
Expiry date is nearing,
Just as skyscrapers are getting taller,
Mother Nature is toppled by the technology king.

A Period of Consequences

Jack Allum-Gruselle, Aged 11

With splinters of the end raining down

Plummeting

On top of some of our last hopes,

I see a blink of light

In this controversy of darkness.

An extra track

At the end of the railway.

Our story so far has been rather bleak;

Mother Earth, our fanatical guardian,

Has some complaints to make

As our beacon of wonder,

Our only home

Is seriously coughing

In the ring of smoke we've caused.

With guzzling engines and repulsive fumes

Adding to mother Earth's fever

Fierce storms of all sorts munch handfuls of victims.

The landmark snows of Kilimanjaro

Perish without sunscreen;

Treacherous and astonishing glaciers

Disappear in a mist of betrayal and confusion

And peaceful icebergs
Dwelling lazily on a calm blue ocean
Trickle away
Into the hands of the heat.

So the seas will flood
The runes and hieroglyphs swallowed
By the greedy mouth of the sea;
Manhattan, Mumbai, Shanghai
And the great half deep city Venice
All shipwrecked at the bottom of the ocean.

The consequences are
That baby bear's porridge is getting too hot.
However the simplest solution is to find
That blink of light
To find that extra track;
When you pray, move your feet,
And always remember
that we can easily solve our mistakes
If we all have the same ones
And if we all march in unison...

Creatures of the Sea

Daisy Teodori-Faith, Aged 11

I speak for those who can not speak

The dolphins tongue.

I speak for the seas you have poisoned

With your rubbish, chemicals and oils.

I speak for the silent seals that get washed up on the shore

And swim no more,

I speak for the whales, citizens of the sea.

Who move peacefully with their family.

I speak for all the suffering creatures of the deep oceans

Who sing their soft, sad songs.

But not for long.

Cry for the Rainforest

Elliot Notley, Aged 9

When the loggers come to town,
Big trees come tumbling down.
These trees are where creatures live,
What in return shall we give?
Trees are being cut faster than we know,
So now where will the creatures go?

We need trees to make oxygen and CO2,
The rainforest gives us many things to study and do.
And oxygen is what we really need,
To help us breathe.
When we find the forest is going,
Our life is slowing and slowing.

The trees are all being cut only 7% remain,
So we must be completely insane.
Indonesia has lost 5.2 million acres,
Just blame the illegal forest takers.

It's got birds, mammals, reptiles and fish,
All sorts of fruits to make a lovely dish.
Branches and leaves burn to the ground,
While animals die without a sound.
When we cut off chunks of wood,

We should be put in jail for not being good.
Every time we cut the trees down,
We should put seeds into the ground.

When parts of the forest change from trees to flames,
The trees must feel a lot of pain.

To walk through it would take many days,
With all sorts of colours from greens to greys.
It's big enough to cover the earth,
If only we realised what it is worth.

The trees cover the sky,
And make enough oxygen for somebody never to die.

When the animals die,
Nobody in the world ever starts to cry.
Which means we don't care,
So when we die it's pretty fair.

When we die,
Don't start to cry,
As we were the people who destroyed the rainforest.

Dead

Freddie Gorst, Aged 10

The car goes past,

The monkey's looking,

Time goes fast with builder's bookings,

Skyscrapers tall, watch rainforests fall,

No time to wait, we've got to escape,

The bulldozers coming,

The animals running,

Tigers, monkeys, lions and all,

Running, running, before the rainforest falls.

Oh no! Oh no! The road ahead,

One split second, the animals....

DEAD!

Dear Person in Charge

Jacob Owen, Aged 8

Dear person in charge,

Stop killing the tigers.

Save the tiger, save the tiger.

Fence out the poachers.

Why are you cutting down the trees?

Save the tiger, save the tiger.

Stop building factories,

Stop using machines.

Save the tiger, save the tiger.

Why are you stealing the tiger's home?

The Destruction of the Elements

Marie Libosvar, Aged 9

Long, long ago,
Rivers would flow,
Through fresh green hills,
Through water mills,
Now they gurgle,
Miserable,
Sad they don't thrive,
To keep fish alive.

Long, long before,
On the open moor,
Rabbits happy,
Hopped merrily,
But now they hide,
They're terrified,
Of the moving metal monsters,
Roaring at all hours.

Long in the past,
The sky was vast,
The air was clean,
The clouds pristine,
Now the clouds are heavy,
With petrol fumes dirty,
Which pollute the air,
Does nobody care?

The Dolphins of Cei Newydd

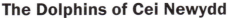

Natasha Gardner, Aged 11

A dark dull day.
The sea and beach are empty
Not a day for the seaside.
Everyone disappointed and sad
Waves lapping onto a deserted beach.

Children moaning and complaining
'Lets walk on the harbour wall' said Dad.
Suddenly they came
First just a splash
Then a fin
Then the smiling grin
Jumping high in the sky.
Then more dolphins came
Cheering up the sea with their beautiful smiles.

Then people started coming
Taking photographs mesmerised.
The Grey day was suddenly sunny.
That night a news reporter
'Drilling to find oil in Cardigan Bay!'
Dolphins and oil don't mix!
A dark dull day again!

Eco-Poem

Luke Proctor, Aged 10

Look all around you,
What do you see?
Because I see the horizon,
But not as it should be.

The grass is going dull,
The trees are going black,
Global warming is upon us,
So we must fight back.

We must win the war that rages
Every day of our life,
But I don't mean violence,
We can't attack with a knife.

What I am saying is,
We must stop pollution
Because we are paying,
For the damage we have done.

But we can redeem ourselves if we try,
And save the last slice of pie,
Which lies on the plate of the universe,
That we call Earth.

The Environment

Chloe Laycock, Aged 11

Sweet wrappers and plastic bags,
Chuck them on the floor,
Packaging and clothes tags,
Polluting the planet to the core!

Car fumes and global warming,
Choking the world with CO2,
Storms and death are a warning,
I'm saying this because it's true!

Trees dying and animals to,
A sky full of smoke,
Trapping the wild in a man made zoo,
What I'm telling you is not a joke!

Gas guzzlers and chuffing cars,
Suffocating the sky,
Fumes blocking out the stars,
We even make the ice caps cry!

Sweet wrappers and plastic bags,
Chuck them on the floor,
Packaging and clothes tags,
Polluting the planet to the core!

The Environment

Charlotte Hall, Aged 9

I am walking through the woods,
It is just the start of spring,
I'm watching flowers grow
And smelling the scent they bring.

The birds are singing their beautiful songs,
And the crystal river flows quietly by.
I see a rainbow shining and floating,
Through the blue suburban sky.

I'm walking through the woods,
On this perfect spring day.
I wish that it could always be this perfect,
Every single day.

Forest Life

Emily Dormand-Bean, Aged 11

The sun awoken at dawn, spreads out its fiery fingers
A glowing spider in the sky

A blanket of silence lifts slowly from the trees
And the forest springs to life, ready, waiting

Animals in their habitat, go about their daily business
Below on the forest floor are secrets, untold

How can an image like this be disturbed?

That's forest life.

Soon the loggers are here and there
The view is destroyed, a picture torn, shredded
Homes gone and the secrets never to be discovered

How can we live on, with this?

That's forest life.

Galloping From Disaster

Jennifer Coppinger, Aged 10

Spring comes like a lily opening.

Bringing birth and sweet merry music.

Up on a high ridge she stands shaking her long creamy mane,

The sun shines on her golden coat

But as the heat rises, she knows she must move on.

Summer comes like a burning sun,

Leaping over boulders in his way,

The burning chestnut crashes onto the earth

Sending bold heat waves though the land,

Shaking his mane as he gallops through fields

Making flowers grow

But as the leaves start falling, he knows he must move on.

Autumn comes like thunder booming across the sky

Leaves fall like rain obeying his command

Scaring the hunters back to their homes.

Feeling on top of the world, he rears, waving his tail in pleasure,

But as the ghostly winter stallion comes,

He knows he must move on.

Winter comes like an icy chill,

Sending birds to migration

He runs through people giving them a terrible shiver,

Sneering and jeering from his high ledge, listening to the icicles rattle,

But as blossom grows on trees, he knows he must move on.

The spirit of these horses want to survive but, when they hear the

crackle of flame and the buzz of chain-saws,

They know they must move on.

His Evil Plan

Mahala Woodhouse, Aged 11

Squish all the spiders
Tear down all the trees
Pulverise the polar bears
Suck up all the seas

Spit on the monkeys
Boil them in a stew
Cut 'em into quarters
And strangle them too

Torture the tigers
Poison the plants
Make humbugs out of panda bears
Squeeze juice out of ants

He goes by the name of pollution
And this is his evil plan
We have to do something to stop him
That is... if we can.

How to Save the Planet

Bertie King, Aged 9

If you want to save the planet, you've got to cut your CO2,
If you think about it, there are lots of things you can do.

At home turn off lights, and close doors to conserve heat,
Put solar panels on your roof and then your house will be complete.

In town buy local food and cut down food miles,
Buy organic and make the planet smile.
If it's not far don't use the car,
That's the solution to cut down pollution.

Don't pollute the rivers or cut down trees,
We all need to save mountains, forests and seas.

If you want to save the planet, then don't burn fossil fuels,
We can all help each other if we follow these simple rules:

REUSE, REDUCE, RECYCLE!

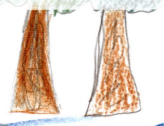

I Give You

Megan Watson, Aged 10

I give you clean beaches,
You give me pollution!

I give you beautiful creatures,
You give me extinction.

Mankind, listen to me!

I give you clean air,
You give me greenhouse gasses.

I give you freedom,
You give me a cage of despair.

Mankind listen to me!

I give you a place where rivers flow,
You give me dams and waterworks.

I give you a place to have fun
You give me a place to die.

Mankind listen to me,
I give you all of these things.
What good things have you given me?

What will I look like in ten year's time?

Into the Future

Shermarke Mohamud, Aged 9

Into the future there are many coloured doors.

Behind the murky brown door,
There is a disgusting horrendous world,
All around there are animals gasping for life,
Dying deer cry with their last breath,
I see poisonous mosquitoes looking for someone to sting,
I can hear rats scuttling,
A whirling tornado smashing the innocent trees,
Bloodsucking bats screeching,
My heart sinks.

Behind the fresh green door
There is a marvellous, magnificent world,
All around there are milky-white waterfalls streaming down,
A marble palace with clean magnificent grounds.
A golden sun shining brightly
A jewel sky sparkling like diamonds,
I can hear canaries tweeting happily in the trees
I am glowing inside.

The Lost Rainforest

Marcus Johnson, Aged 10

For thousands of years you've
Stood proud and tall,
Providing oxygen for us all.

Left on your own
you flourished and spread,
through mans interference
you're now almost dead.

The animals that
lived where your canopy fell,
have now had to find
other places to dwell.

Man should have realised
your immense worth,
How important you are
to our earth.

Cutting you down
was the wrong thing to do.
It is something we have
come to rue.

If we left you alone you would
again spread yourself out,
This is something of which we have no doubt.

My Magic Box

James Green, Aged 9

My magic box contains:

The football skills of Cristiano Ronaldo,

The first step of a toddler,

The thirteenth month of the year,

The smell of lovely chicken breasts in the oven,

The taste of mayo on a sandwich,

The last bark of my dog, Sandie,

The first tooth I had,

The mind of J. K. Rowling,

The smile of a baby when a present is opened,

The first time I swam.

My Views on the Environment

Gemma Wise, Aged 9

The environment is very special to me.

As I love both the land and the sea.

I wish that people would be aware,

That dropping litter is not fair.

It makes the land look an utter mess,

As well as putting all the animals under stress.

Destroying our land such as a forest or a wood,

I do not think is very good,

Because all the wildlife now, has nowhere to go.

When will it end? I would love to know.

Be careful out there, I make this plea.

I do hope that you all agree!

Once Upon A Time

Hannah Phillips, Aged 10

Once upon a time
Life was great
The sun was never early
Nor was it late

Flowers and plants
Rivers and seas
Rocks and boulders
And the tallest trees

Once upon a time
The world was itself
Spinning on axis
It's own kind of wealth

Then we came
And how did it change
War and capture
Torture and pain

Then arrived another
The cloud of what we are
Hotels and shops
Buildings and cars

_____

Scientific and amazing
It may be
The ice caps are melting
That's one thing to see

Warmth and fumes
Has filled the air
Our planet is dying
That's one thing to see

Once upon a time
No fear of our selves
Electricity should be windmills
And taps could be wells

We still have the chance
To live properly again
Use it now
Like we did then

Once upon a time
Is a dream come true
Want it to happen?
It's up to you.

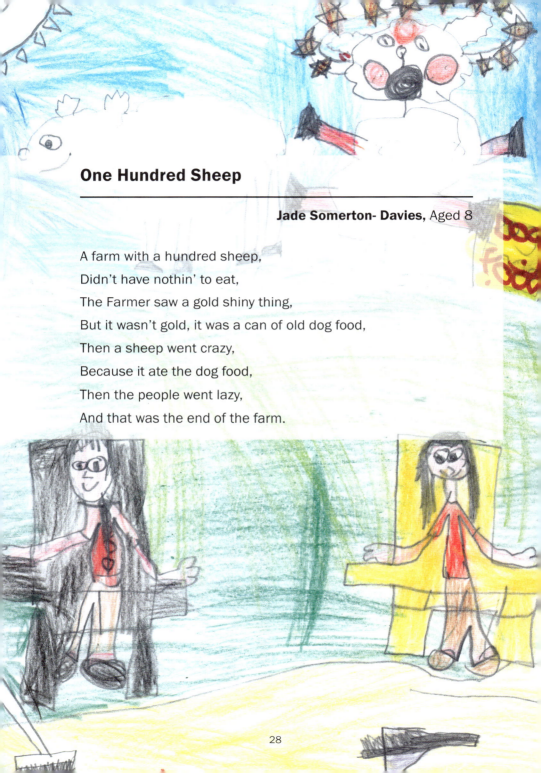

One Hundred Sheep

Jade Somerton- Davies, Aged 8

A farm with a hundred sheep,

Didn't have nothin' to eat,

The Farmer saw a gold shiny thing,

But it wasn't gold, it was a can of old dog food,

Then a sheep went crazy,

Because it ate the dog food,

Then the people went lazy,

And that was the end of the farm.

Our Planet

Ben Allen, Aged 9

Pandas chewing,
Troubles brewing,
Trees blazing,
Water levels raising,

Animals hunted,
Gorillas grunted,
Thunder and lightning,
How frightening,

Trees falling,
Animals brawling,
People mauling,
Rainforests falling,

Butterflies flying,
Land owners buying,
Bee's buzzing,
Cars brumming,
Monkeys swinging in the trees,
With the busy buzzing bees.

Our Planet

Courtney Marchant, Aged 11

Every day our planet gets warmer
The icebergs melt and the sea gets taller.

The Summers get longer and Winters get shorter,
And Autumn and Spring won't be with us much longer.

We must stop burning fossil fuel,
Or our kids future will be pretty cruel.

Let's start walking or catch buses or trains,
Or the future will go down the drain.

Let's recycle and watch our waste,
Or in 20 odd years there'll be a nasty taste.

We must build wind farms to produce our power,
To make sure that the future will flower.

So come on everybody start helping, on the double,
Because if you don't we'll be in big trouble!!!!!!

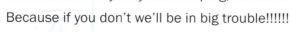

Our World in Your Hands

Oliver Welland, Aged 11

The Earth is crumbling,
The earth is weak.
And we are all watching ,
From high mountain peaks.

"So help us to live!"
I cried to the men.
I screamed and I showed them,
A dark and damp den.

There a frail old woman,
All beaten and weak,
Has given us so much,
Now your kindness she seeks.

I cried " This is our mother,
The mother of all.
The mother of Spring,
Summer ,Winter and Fall."

One world, one home,
It started at our birth.
Land and man in harmony,
All children of Mother Earth.

Penguins at Risk

Luke Elwood, Aged 9

Soon my homeland will be gone
And me too.
The ice will crack
And I shall fall.
My future is running out
For I will be no more.

The glistening ice that I love
Will be wiped out.
The seas will rise,
Waves will crash and
Flood my land.
This could be my last day.

My life is worth nothing,
It could be,
But humans will kill me anyway.
I don't want to die.

Planet Destruction

Thomas Stonehouse & Nathan Bingley, Aged 11

A is for atmosphere, the gas surrounding the earth.

B is for bins overflowing and smelly.

C is for cars pumping out clouds.

D is for dump, wasting products and food.

E is for electricity that heats up our planet.

F is for farmers who spray their crops.

G is for global warming.

H is for habitats of our wildlife.

I is for ignorance, not knowing how to help.

J is for jumbo jet plane using gallons of fuel.

K is for kitchen with CFC fridges.

L is for life preserving - not extinction.

M is for monster trucks with their big exhausts.

N is for nicotine to damage our lungs.

O is for oil slick that dirties our seas.

P is for paper we take from our trees.

Q is for quiet that we hope for.

R is for rubbish that litters the streets.

S is for sewers all smelly and overflowing.

T is for traffic, too much on the roads.

U is for ultra-violet rays of the sun.

V is for vandalism all around our world.

W is for water we are wasting.

X is for x-ray with radiation waves.

Y is for youth suffering the effects of today.

Z is for zinc batteries that leak out their liquid.

Planet Earth

Alice Johnstone, Aged 10

Where rivers used to flow,
There are now polluted streams,
Where rainforests used to grow.
There are now the stumps of trees.

The planet is decaying,
Before our very eyes,
But it is with our actions,
We can help it to survive.

The sea levels are now rising,
Faster than we can control,
And fossil fuels are being burnt
Such as oil, diesel and coal.

With global warming setting in,
We must all work together,
Otherwise we are at risk,
Of losing the Earth forever.

With the ice in both poles melting,
Polar bears and penguins will die,
Now the rest of the world is sweltering,
To save the Earth we must try.

Carbon dioxide in the atmosphere,
Is creating a blanket around the Earth,
It's getting steadily hotter year by year,
Changing from bad to worse.

Recycling will help to save,
The rotting world we live in,
All the energy we crave,
We must cut down or give in.

There are many wars on this Earth,
Such as World War I and II,
But the real war is between climate change and the planet,
Who will win is up to you.

Across the world many tongues are spoken,
But we must learn to co-operate,
We have many different languages,
Yet we share one planet and its fate.

We dream of science fiction,
Monsters who destroy and invade,
But are we not the real monsters,
Who may leave no Earth to save?

The Polar Bear

Grace O'Brien, Aged 10

We Kings of the ice, the polar bears,
Hunt our pray whilst they are unaware.
We roam our land without a care,
Other creatures must beware!

The glistening sun can be quite a glare,
The beautiful landscape is becoming rare.
Feathery-white snow flutters through the air,
So bold the ice in the summer heat's flare.

Our life now, is quite unfair,
The ice is thinning, becoming a scare!
Cubs are suffering everywhere,
Finding food is impossible to bear...

Why is life so unfair?

Will we be able to repair,
The damage that you have declared?
Carbon dioxide into the air, Is causing terror and despair.

Our species is becoming desperately rare,
But none of you seem to care...
Will anyone save the last of us,
We Kings of the ice, the polar bears?

Precious World

Paige Hunt, Aged 9

Slippery slimy oil
in a crystal blue sea.

Smokey black exhaust
in the fresh Spring air.

Smelly rusty beer cans
in a green grassy meadow.

Thick factory smoke
wafting in front of the sunrise.

Hazardous chemicals dumped
on a living river bank.

Make no more pollution
in our unique precious world!

The Rainforest

Celine Stretton, Aged 10

In the density of the leaves,
A coiling python weaves,
In and out of the trees and flowers.
Can anyone doubt the rainforest's powers?

In the humidity, a community thrives,
Frogs with green luminous eyes.
An army of ants, almighty and strong,
A chorus of birds chirruping a song.

The leaves are as green as green can be,
A rainbow of colours is what I see.
But I turn around and what do I find?
A whole different scene cripples my mind.

The trees are being chopped down,
And emptiness is all around.
A parrot caws its lonesome cry,
A frog springs from a leaf nearby.

The decades of trees are chopped down in seconds,
As for the animals and plants, death beckons.
The end of this mighty forest is near,
The moral of the story is surely now clear.

So let us find,
In our selfish minds,
What everyone can do,
And you can help too,
To save the rainforest from destruction.

The Recycled Poem

Amber Draper, Aged 11

I wondered why the lonely cloud
Was polluting the high vales and hills,
When all at once I saw a crowd
Stamping on the golden daffodils;
Beside the polluted lake, Beneath the blackened trees,
A crisp packet fluttering and dancing in the breeze.

Continuous as the old tin cans that shine
And twinkle along the motorway,
They stretched in a never ending line
In the waves being washed up in the bay.
Ten thousand saw I at a glance
Rattling their heads in a sprightly dance.

(After William Wordsworth.
I have 'recycled' it to be more realistic for our Earth today)

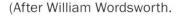

40

Reuse, Recycle , Reduce

Charlotte Francis, Aged 11

We've been working on recycling
All the trash we can,
We've been working on recycling,
It's a very simple plan,
Separate your glass and paper,
Separate your plastic and tin.
Take the trash that you've recycled
To your recycling bin.

We've been working on reducing
All the trash we can.
We've been working on reducing
It's a very simple plan.
Don't go wasting any products,
Just use exactly what you need.
Don't buy things in extra wrapping
Reduce and you'll succeed.

We've been working on reusing
All the trash we can.
We've been working on reusing:
It's a very simple plan.
If it's a paper bag you're using,
Don't use it once, don't use it twice!
Give old clothes and toys to someone, to reuse them would be nice!

Save our Planet

Martin Walker, Aged 10

The tall, proud trees, their leaves fluttering in the breeze.

The peaceful forest rustling with woodland creatures.

The tiny chirping birds majestically singing.

But We, slash down the trees, tear down the bird nests

and destroy creature's habitats with destructive machines.

The peaceful meadow, crawling with insects, home of the farmer's cow.

But We, plough all the grass and crush all the insect's homes.

The quiet ponds and squishy marshes, breathing with life.

The slimy frogs live in the marshes and sway in the ponds.

But We, drain all the ponds and munch the frog's habitats.

The magnificent shimmering ocean, swaying waves jumping on top.

Multi-coloured fish, majestically playing under water.

But We, poison the water with choking chemicals,

Wreck the food chain and kill the fish with suffocating gases.

The glimmering lakes and tarns, peacefully swaying with glittery fish.

On scorching hot summer's days we like to swim in these lakes.

But We poison the water, kill all the fish and drain the beautiful lakes.

The delicate, stunning ice caps, home of the fierce polar bears.

Cold as a frozen snow man.

The polar bears splash their paws into the water

and violently munch the fish.

But we crush all the ice, leave the polar bears stranded

and melt the ice with destructive chemical gases

WE MUST ACT NOW!!!

Save Our Trees, People and Animals

Charlie Parry, Aged 9

Save our trees,
Green rock hard trees,
They stare at us all day,
Keeping our oxygen clean,
Don't cut them down.

Home for birds and bugs,
The red and brown birds
And green gravely bugs,
Innocent animals not at war.

No more pine cones,
No more shade,
Keep the chainsaws at bay,
Let the trees see another day.

If the trees go,
We will go,
The animals will go,
The beautiful animals.

Say good-bye to your furry hats,
Say good-bye to your silly cats
Say good-bye to your dirty dogs,
Say good-bye to your slimy frogs.

You will loose all these things if the trees are gone.

The Seasons

Molly Ellen Turecek, Aged 10

Spring approaches and scatters all around us
Bringing birth and sweet sounds
The soft light catches swifts crossing the sky
Such splendour, true colours awaken
But then summer tramples on the spring flowers.

Summer appears leaping with joy
The wrinkly nuts crash onto earth
Bold heat waves flash across the land
Images of cars flashing in front of us
But summer eventually dies.

Autumn comes like a rocket in the sky
Trees arching over like weeping willows
And leaves stumbling at our feet
The wind howling at the earth
But the mist covers up autumn and winter is born.

Winter covers the earth
And its crystal white moon sails across the gloomy sky
The trees shiver with its bare branches
But then it soon gets tucked away
And will come out another day.

Our wonderful seasons keep spinning
But how long can this carry on?
We are corrupting and smothering this precious gift
Forcing our seasons into confusion.
One day it could stop, just like a human heart.

Spring

Harry Hetherington-Aherne, Aged 8

It's roar draws the forest to a halt,
It bears it's teeth to see animals turn away,
His mane shakes and winter dies,
He gives joy of new life.

Animals honour him,
For his slendour and true colours,
He doesn't choose sides,
For war is his nemesis.

Why Oh Why he thinks,
Did the world of evil dawn,
For all he wants is to bloom,
In eternal hopeful life.

He dies and summer is born,
But comes to life again,
Without him new beginnings,
Would surely not be here.

The Storm

Kyle Redublo, Aged 8

Without warning,
A werewolf of dark cloud rises in the gloomy sky.
It roars as it glides and spreads its dark,
The moon covered the mountain is bright,
Far away is heard the shout of the werewolf.

Up rushes the storm,
Is dark,
Its teeth is mouthlike, a wild beast,
The rattling moment after the iron chain,
And it uses his fire to blow and it uses his mouth to eat people.

Time's Ticking Away

George Davies, Aged 11

Cool calm waters,
Street lights glowing,
Stars shining -
Glory in the wind.

In the distance,
A sea family
Splashing through the waves.
Underneath them,
Fifteen thousand tentacles
Of the ocean stinger.

Above me,
Flashing winds blow,
Dancing through the moonlight
The sun rises,
Hills glowing,
Trees standing tall
While morning begins.

Colour plants
A reflection on the water.
A garden of love grows.
The sunlight starts to go dim.
A thin forest awakens
and a path through the middle,
A monkey climbs and grips a branch,
Looks behind for trouble.

The sun crows
with darkness on the field.
Time's ticking away.
Time's running out.
Darkness.
What's happened to earth?

Tonyrefail

Riva Vatsaloo, Aged 11

Tonyrefail means to me,
An amazing view of green rolling hills
As I see the giant white windmills,
They stand up tall they stand up proud
like daffodils up in the clouds,
With the great welsh mountains as their background.

Tonyrefail means to me,
The Ely river running strong,
It twists and snakes and bubbles along
Coedely colliery is now a memory,
That was once a place of activity
Where miners went to dig the coal
Known as Tonyrefail gold.

Tonyrefail means to me.
A place to see my family
A place where I feel I belong,
A place where all my friends are from
A place that I can call my home,
A place I never feel alone.

That's what Tonyrefail means to me.

Urban Jungle

Joseph Devoy, Aged 11

The Elephant prowls through his jungle
Awaiting the humans' presence.
No one is here except him and the trees.
He looks around at the decaying jungle.
He doesn't understand his pain.

The trees are dying
The Elephant's crying.
Is this the final dawning?

No one to play with. No one to have fun.
Not even a soul. He's all alone.
And then they come crowding round.
Making the jungle cry.
The Elephant stares, he understands.

He rages and rampages.
Fire flows instead of blood.
His anger rises and becomes what they fear.
It is too much to bear.
Flying, crying, he chokes for air.
And realizes he is just their entertainment.

The trees are dying
The Elephant's crying.
Is this the final dawning?

More come with weapons.
They come for war.
To hurt the world a bit more.
And he looks at where they come from.
And rushes at the door.

He runs alone the concrete jungle.
The urban environment.
Everything slows down and goes silent.
His head is numb but he keeps running.

The trees are dying
The Elephant's crying.
Is this the final dawning?

He tumbles to the ground.
All he wants is peace.
He lies down to sleep.
He's finally in his jungle.
He sleeps and sleeps and sleeps.

Ways of Looking at Endangered Animals

Sam Hughes, Aged 10

Elephants may squirt you with water
But that does not give the right to slaughter.

Gorillas beat their chests as hard as they can
But that is stopping for the right of man.

Pandas love their bamboo.
But the bamboo is dying and the pandas are too.

Rhinos come in black and white,
But more and more do not see the light.

The polar bears love the snow,
But the bears seem to come and go.

The tiger is the biggest cat ever,
But who will remember when they have gone forever.

Birds rule the sky,
But that is stopping as more and more die.

We know all of God's creatures' names.
So why should we stop those amazing fames.

They rule the sea, sky and land.
It is like we should be under their command.

They keep our world alive,
So do not let them run and hide.

Even if they're all alone,
Remember they have lives of their own.

They may be wild and crazy
But we are worse - we are lazy.

From the meat eaters to the leaf eaters
They keep our planet alive.

What is More Important?

Jordannah Rees, Aged 9

On the day that I was born
An angel came to me
She talked about times long ago
And how things used to be.

She talked of all the animals
Running wild and free
I caught a glimmer of a smile
She passed it on to me.

I saw a baby lion
A hunter by his side
The fear in it's little face
Made me want to cry .

We talked about the fishes
Swimming in the sea
We talked about the factories
And how they choke the trees.

She took me on a journey
That lasted for a mile
She showed me animals in captivity
And a child without her smile.

We wandered through the houses
Looking deep inside
And there we saw a family
Recycling with pride.

I looked up at the angel
A tear was falling down
I asked why her smile
Had turned into a frown.

She told me of a peaceful place
Which sadly is no more
Instead we live with cruelty
With waste and threats of war.

The moral of this story
I think you would agree
The world would be a better place
If people cared like you and me.

Will for the Earth

Jacob Gray, Aged 11

The smoke shall rise,
It's the Devil's prize.
The trees shall fall,
When they should stand tall.
A few tigers roar,
But there should be more.
And I'd like to keep this Earth.

The majestic macaw soars through the air,
Hunting through rivers, the fierce brown bear,
The manatee seeks food in the shallow of the sea,
The gorilla seeks refuge in the shadow of a tree.
These animals are the ones that I'd like to keep,
But I can only dream about them as I sleep.
As man, and cars and all his pollution,
Are destroying the Earth's evolution.

When I see the view from the top of the hill,
All the beautiful things change my will,
I'll stop,
I'll change,
I'll help keep the earth alive,
So all its creatures shall thrive and thrive.

The Wooden Giant

Daniel Wrigley, Aged 10

As the wind blows, my green hands flourish on the breeze,

Birds sing in my arms,

Monkeys clamber around me,

The calls of men echo in my mind,

As the metal chain rips me open,

Animals scatter in fear,

Now I die on the forest floor,

As a habitat for small creatures,

Whilst I rot away in Mother Nature's arms.

Index

**You must be the change
you want to see in the world**

Mahatma Gandhi (1869 - 1948)